THE ARTHURIAN ADDRESS BOOK

To Felicity Aldridge and Paul Brady,
true friends and loyal supporters.

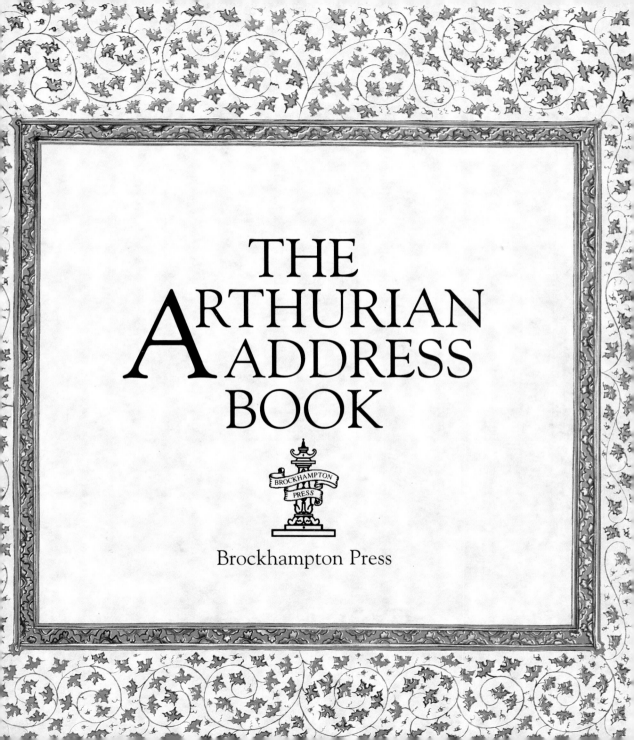

THE
ARTHURIAN
ADDRESS
BOOK

Brockhampton Press

ADDRESS BOOK

First published in Great Britain in 1997 by Brockhampton Press,
a member of Hodder Headline PLC Group,
20 Bloomsbury Street, London WC1B 3QA

ISBN 1 86019 426 5

An Eddison·Sadd Edition
Edited, designed and produced by
Eddison Sadd Editions Limited
St Chad's House, 148 King's Cross Road
London WC1X 9DH

Phototypeset in Goudy Old Style using QuarkXpress on Apple Macintosh
Origination by Columbia Offset, Singapore
Printed by BPC Dunstable, United Kingdom

THE LANDS ADVENTUROUS

In one of the most famous medieval Arthurian romances, Perlesvaus or The High History of the Holy Grail, *the author breaks off his narrative to remark upon the fact that the lands of Britain – in Arthur's day known as Logres – possessed the property of never remaining the same. No matter how often the knights rode forth in search of wrongs to right, the roads they followed always led to new challenges and tests in the 'Lands Adventurous'.*

Within these lands lived people who forsook human company because their way of life stemmed from a more ancient time: these were the faery women, the dwarfs, the magicians and enchantresses. Holy hermits also lived there, whose duty it was to maintain tiny enclaves of sanctuary, to which might come wounded animals, lost travellers, knights injured in combat or repentant villains.

Within this world of forest and mountain, threaded by river and bound by the sea, were the castles and courts: places of civilization and repose, wherein dwelt the king and his nobles, their wives, mistresses, knights, squires, servants and soldiers. The knights travelled between one court and another, riding forth as emissary, quester or champion. Thus might we find Sir Lancelot, sleeping beneath a shady tree in the heat of noon, until four magical queens, riding by under the shade of a silken canopy, sought to capture him. Or we might follow the footsteps of Sir Gawain, riding in the heart of winter through 'the wilderness of Wirrall', in search of the mysterious Green Chapel, sleeping in his armour on the frost-bound earth, glad of the sight of the lights of a castle shining forth in the darkness.

These magical places – forest and castle, fountain and sea-shore – form the substance of the Arthurian world, for the locations were as important as the people who lived there. If they had possessed address books such as the one you now hold, they might well have recorded 'the Black Knight, who dwells hard by the Fountain of Baranton, in the Forest of Broceliande'. As it is, story-tellers through the ages have recorded these places for us, making them real for all time.

Caitlín and John Matthews

AMESBURY. *Queen Guinevere came to this great monastic house during the war between Arthur and Mordred. And, when the King had departed for Avalon, there she died and was laid to rest in a marble tomb. Sir Lancelot, who had become a hermit, arrived but a half hour after her death and, broken hearted, sang a mass and conducted the service for her burial the next day.*

Name

Address

Telephone

Name

Address

Telephone

Name

Address

Telephone

Name

Address

Telephone

Name

Address

Telephone

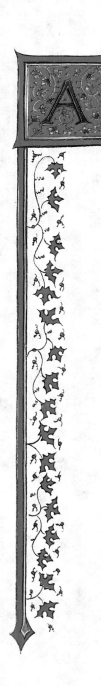

Name

Address

Telephone

Name

Address

Telephone

Name

Address

Telephone

Name

Address

Telephone

Name

Address

Telephone

Name
Address

Telephone

Name
Address

Telephone

Name
Address

Telephone

Name
Address

Telephone

Name
Address

Telephone

Name

Address

Telephone

Name

Address

Telephone

Name

Address

Telephone

Name

Address

Telephone

Name

Address

Telephone

BRANGANE. *This lady was the handmaid to Isolt of Ireland. She sailed with her mistress to Cornwall, where Isolt was to marry King Mark. On the voyage, Isolt and the hero Tristan accidentally drank a love potion intended for Isolt and Mark. To disguise the fact that her mistress was no longer a virgin, Brangane took the place of Isolt on the wedding night. Brangane continued to serve her lady well, as in this scene, where she carries a secret letter from Isolt to Tristan.*

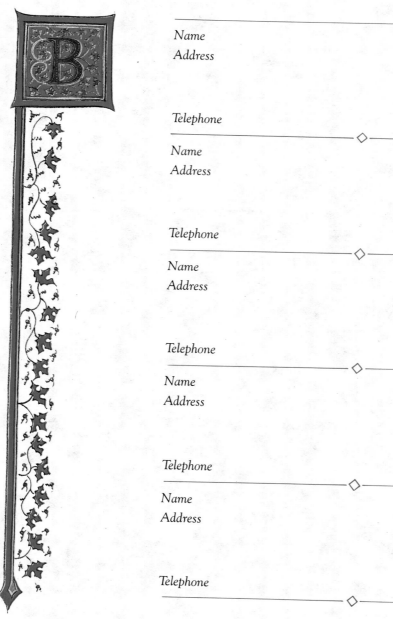

Name

Address

Telephone

Name

Address

Telephone

Name

Address

Telephone

Name

Address

Telephone

Name

Address

Telephone

Name

Address

Telephone

Name

Address

Telephone

Name

Address

Telephone

Name

Address

Telephone

Name

Address

Telephone

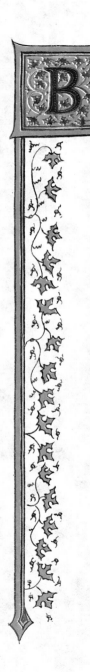

Name

Address

Telephone

Name

Address

Telephone

Name

Address

Telephone

Name

Address

Telephone

Name

Address

Telephone

Name

Address

Telephone

Name

Address

Telephone

Name

Address

Telephone

Name

Address

Telephone

Name

Address

Telephone

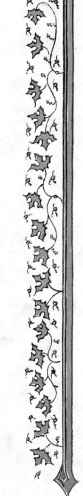

CAERLEON. Also called by its Roman name 'The City of the Legions', Caerleon is located on the River Usk in Monmouthshire, Wales. It was the second-greatest city in all of Arthur's kingdom. Here he held court in great splendour, and here, after his wars with an alliance of rebel kings, he first wore the crown of the realm upon his head. Although the new city of Camelot became more famous in later years, Arthur always loved to return to the scene of his first great triumph.

Name

Address

Telephone

Name

Address

Telephone

Name

Address

Telephone

Name

Address

Telephone

Name

Address

Telephone

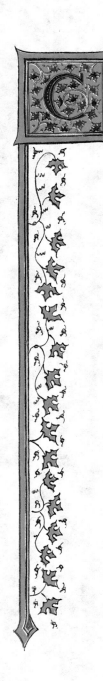

Name
Address

Telephone

Name
Address

Telephone

Name
Address

Telephone

Name
Address

Telephone

Name
Address

Telephone

Name

Address

Telephone

Name

Address

Telephone

Name

Address

Telephone

Name

Address

Telephone

Name

Address

Telephone

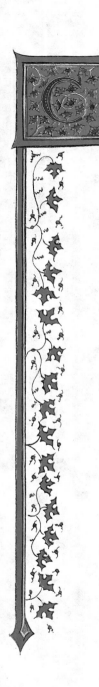

Name

Address

Telephone

Name

Address

Telephone

Name

Address

Telephone

Name

Address

Telephone

Name

Address

Telephone

Name

Address

Telephone

Name

Address

Telephone

Name

Address

Telephone

Name

Address

Telephone

Name

Address

Telephone

DINDRAINE. This lady was sister to the great knight Sir Perceval. She lived a most devout and holy life until she was twenty years old, at which time she joined her brother and his companions in the Quest for the Holy Grail. During their journey together they encountered a castle where a leprous lady demanded the blood of a virgin to heal her. Dindraine willingly gave her blood, but died as a result and was laid to rest in the City of the Grail when the Quest ended.

Name

Address

Telephone

Name

Address

Telephone

Name

Address

Telephone

Name

Address

Telephone

Name

Address

Telephone

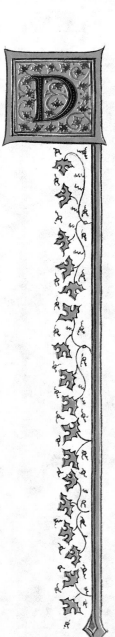

Name

Address

Telephone

⬦

Name

Address

Telephone

⬦

Name

Address

Telephone

⬦

Name

Address

Telephone

⬦

Name

Address

Telephone

⬦

Name

Address

Telephone

Name

Address

Telephone

Name

Address

Telephone

Name

Address

Telephone

Name

Address

Telephone

Name

Address

Telephone

Name

Address

Telephone

Name

Address

Telephone

Name

Address

Telephone

Name

Address

Telephone

Name

Address

Telephone

Name

Address

Telephone

Name

Address

Telephone

Name

Address

Telephone

Name

Address

Telephone

EXCALIBUR. Arthur's mighty and magical sword was the gift of the Lady of the Lake during the first months of his reign. It was said that while he held it, no one could defeat him in battle; and, as long as he kept the scabbard, he could not be hurt. The scabbard, however, was stolen by Morgan le Fay and, after the terrible battle at Camlan in which Arthur and Mordred wounded each other unto death, the sword itself was returned to the lake from whence it came.

Name
Address

Telephone
Name
Address

Telephone
Name
Address

Telephone
Name
Address

Telephone
Name
Address

Telephone

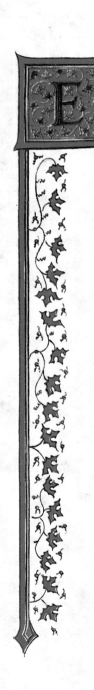

Name

Address

Telephone

Name

Address

Telephone

Name

Address

Telephone

Name

Address

Telephone

Name

Address

Telephone

Name

Address

Telephone

Name

Address

Telephone

Name

Address

Telephone

Name

Address

Telephone

Name

Address

Telephone

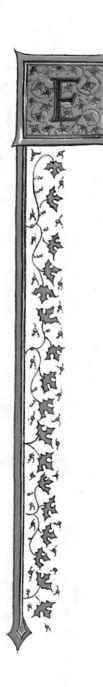

Name

Address

Telephone

Name

Address

Telephone

Name

Address

Telephone

Name

Address

Telephone

Name

Address

Telephone

THE LADY OF THE
FOUNTAIN. *The Black
Knight was the guardian of
a magical fountain deep in
the Forest of Broceliande.
His wife was the Lady of
the Fountain, a woman of
great character and beauty.
When he met his death at
the hands of the youthful
Sir Owain, she was close to
madness from grief.*

*However, when her
maiden, Luned, brought
Owain to her as a suitor,
the Lady of the Fountain
fell in love with him almost
at once. They were soon
married and the young hero
became the new guardian
of the fountain. The two
dwelt in peace together for
many years thereafter.*

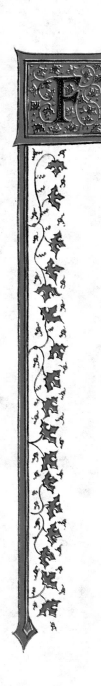

Name

Address

Telephone

Name

Address

Telephone

Name

Address

Telephone

Name

Address

Telephone

Name

Address

Telephone

Name

Address

Telephone

Name

Address

Telephone

Name

Address

Telephone

Name

Address

Telephone

Name

Address

Telephone

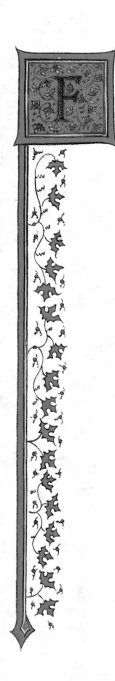

Name

Address

Telephone

Name

Address

Telephone

Name

Address

Telephone

Name

Address

Telephone

Name

Address

Telephone

Name

Address

Telephone

Name

Address

Telephone

Name

Address

Telephone

Name

Address

Telephone

Name

Address

Telephone

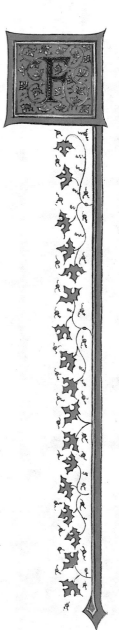

GAWAIN. Arthur's nephew, Sir Gawain of Orkney, was the greatest knight ever to sit at the Round Table – save perhaps Sir Lancelot. Of Gawain's many adventures, the most notable were when he successfully accepted the Green Knight's challenge; and when he won the love of the Lady Ragnall who was enchanted in hideous form until he gave her the right to choose the shape that she would retain.

Name

Address

Telephone

Name

Address

Telephone

Name

Address

Telephone

Name

Address

Telephone

Name

Address

Telephone

Name

Address

Telephone

Name

Address

Telephone

Name

Address

Telephone

Name

Address

Telephone

Name

Address

Telephone

Name

Address

Telephone

Name

Address

Telephone

Name

Address

Telephone

Name

Address

Telephone

Name

Address

Telephone

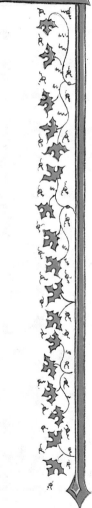

Name

Address

Telephone

Name

Address

Telephone

Name

Address

Telephone

Name

Address

Telephone

Name

Address

Telephone

Name

Address

Telephone

Name

Address

Telephone

Name

Address

Telephone

Name

Address

Telephone

Name

Address

Telephone

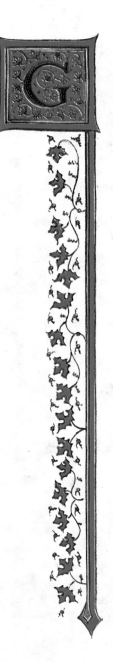

HERMIT. *Throughout the long months of the Quest for the Holy Grail, the Knights of the Round Table found help at the hands of the hermits who came to dwell in the Forest of Adventure. Many found rest and refreshment in the poor huts of the hermits, none more so than Sir Lancelot, who finally confessed his long and illicit love for Queen Guinevere to a holy man, from whom he received penance and the courage to continue in the Quest.*

Name
Address

Telephone

Name
Address

Telephone

Name
Address

Telephone

Name
Address

Telephone

Name
Address

Telephone

Name

Address

Telephone

Name

Address

Telephone

Name

Address

Telephone

Name

Address

Telephone

Name

Address

Telephone

Name

Address

Telephone

Name

Address

Telephone

Name

Address

Telephone

Name

Address

Telephone

Name

Address

Telephone

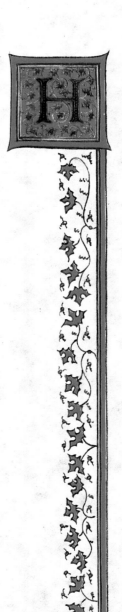

Name

Address

Telephone

Name

Address

Telephone

Name

Address

Telephone

Name

Address

Telephone

Name

Address

Telephone

ISOLT. *Save for Queen Guinevere herself, Isolt of Ireland was the most beautiful woman in all of Arthur's realm. Destined to be the bride of King Mark of Cornwall, she met and fell in love with Tristan of Lyonesse. The two became lovers and faced discovery and death many times. In the end, Isolt fled with her lover to Lancelot's castle of Joyous Garde, where Tristan was later murdered. She did not long outlive him, but flung herself to her death from a high cliff.*

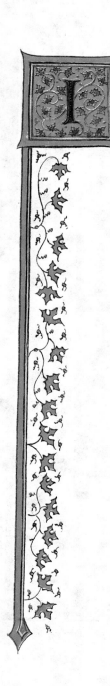

Name

Address

Telephone

Name

Address

Telephone

Name

Address

Telephone

Name

Address

Telephone

Name

Address

Telephone

Name

Address

Telephone

Name

Address

Telephone

Name

Address

Telephone

Name

Address

Telephone

Name

Address

Telephone

Name

Address

Telephone

Name

Address

Telephone

Name

Address

Telephone

Name

Address

Telephone

Name

Address

Telephone

Name

Address

Telephone

Name

Address

Telephone

Name

Address

Telephone

Name

Address

Telephone

Name

Address

Telephone

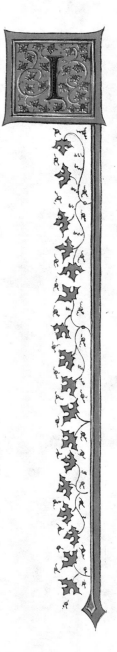

JOYOUS GARDE. *This was Lancelot's castle, said to have stood on the coast of Northumberland. He won it after a great feat of arms when he found words engraved in the lid of a stone tomb which told him of his own ancestry and right to the castle. Until then it had been called Dolorous Garde; but Lancelot changed its name. Although he was seldom within its walls, it gave shelter to Tristan and Isolt after they fled from Cornwall.*

Name
Address

Telephone

Name
Address

Telephone

Name
Address

Telephone

Name
Address

Telephone

Name
Address

Telephone

Name

Address

Telephone

Name

Address

Telephone

Name

Address

Telephone

Name

Address

Telephone

Name

Address

Telephone

Name

Address

Telephone

Name

Address

Telephone

Name

Address

Telephone

Name

Address

Telephone

Name

Address

Telephone

Name

Address

Telephone

Name

Address

Telephone

Name

Address

Telephone

Name

Address

Telephone

Name

Address

Telephone

Name

Address

Telephone

Name

Address

Telephone

Name

Address

Telephone

Name

Address

Telephone

Name

Address

Telephone

THE KNIGHTS OF THE GRAIL. *The Knights of the Round Table braved many long and difficult trials, but none more so than the Quest for the Holy Grail. When the vessel, believed to have been used to celebrate the Last Supper, first appeared at Camelot, every knight sought to undertake the adventure. However, only three succeeded in finding their way to the sacred city of the Grail; and only two others, Gawain and Lancelot, caught more than a glimpse of the shining cup.*

Name

Address

Telephone ◇

Name

Address

Telephone ◇

Name

Address

Telephone ◇

Name

Address

Telephone ◇

Name

Address

Telephone ◇

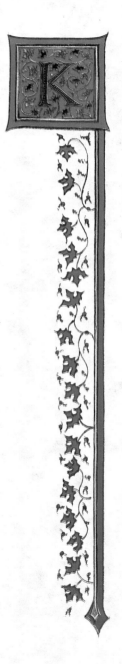

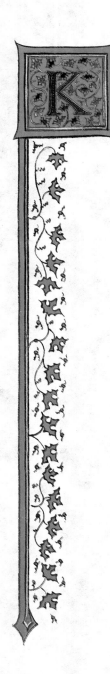

Name

Address

Telephone

Name

Address

Telephone

Name

Address

Telephone

Name

Address

Telephone

Name

Address

Telephone

Name

Address

Telephone

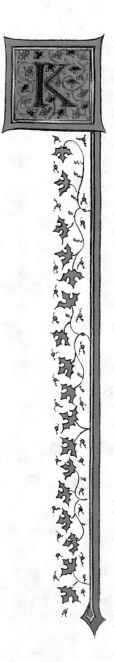

Name

Address

Telephone

Name

Address

Telephone

Name

Address

Telephone

Name

Address

Telephone

K

Name

Address

Telephone

Name

Address

Telephone

Name

Address

Telephone

Name

Address

Telephone

Name

Address

Telephone

LANCELOT. *Considered by all men to be the greatest of the Round Table Knights, Lancelot was brought up by the Otherworldly Lady of the Lake. His love affair with Arthur's queen, Guinevere, became a central cause in the breaking of the Fellowship of the Table. The relationship was often stormy, as in the incident depicted here, where Lancelot, forced to ride in a cart to rescue her, was vilified by Guinevere for not hastening more swiftly to her aid.*

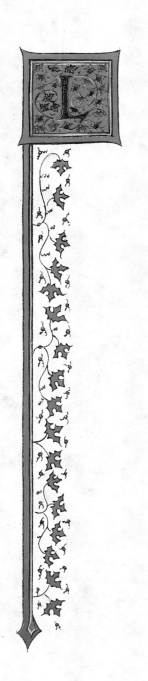

Name

Address

Telephone

Name

Address

Telephone

Name

Address

Telephone

Name

Address

Telephone

Name

Address

Telephone

Name
Address

Telephone

⋄

Name
Address

Telephone

⋄

Name
Address

Telephone

⋄

Name
Address

Telephone

⋄

Name
Address

Telephone

⋄

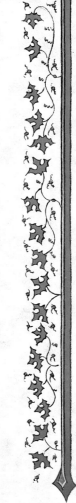

Name

Address

Telephone

Name

Address

Telephone

Name

Address

Telephone

Name

Address

Telephone

Name

Address

Telephone

Name

Address

Telephone

Name

Address

Telephone

Name

Address

Telephone

Name

Address

Telephone

Name

Address

Telephone

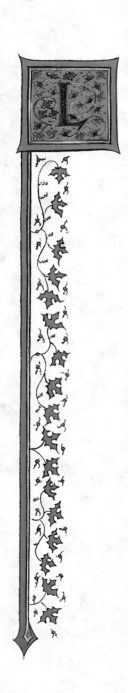

Name

Address

Telephone

Name

Address

Telephone

Name

Address

Telephone

Name

Address

Telephone

Name

Address

Telephone

MERLIN. *The prime mover in the establishment of the Arthurian kingdom, Merlin was believed by some to have come to Britain as one of the last remaining survivors of drowned Atlantis. Others, who were suspicious of his magic and power, told a different story. To them he was the offspring of a devil, saved by the timely intervention of a holy hermit, but retaining the dark power of the Otherworld.*

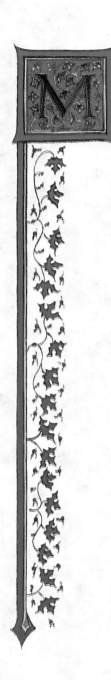

Name

Address

Telephone

Name

Address

Telephone

Name

Address

Telephone

Name

Address

Telephone

Name

Address

Telephone

Name
Address

Telephone

Name
Address

Telephone

Name
Address

Telephone

Name
Address

Telephone

Name
Address

Telephone

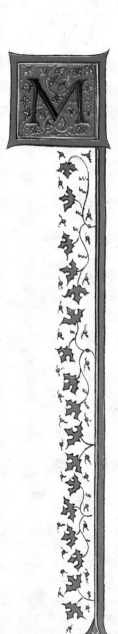

Name

Address

Telephone

Name

Address

Telephone

Name

Address

Telephone

Name

Address

Telephone

Name

Address

Telephone

Name

Address

Telephone

Name

Address

Telephone

Name

Address

Telephone

Name

Address

Telephone

Name

Address

Telephone

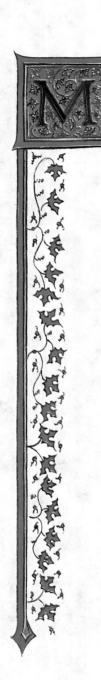

Name

Address

Telephone

Name

Address

Telephone

Name

Address

Telephone

Name

Address

Telephone

Name

Address

Telephone

NIMUE. *The daughter of a royal huntsman named Dionas, Nimue came to the Arthurian court when she was but fifteen years of age, though wise beyond her years. Merlin fell in love with her at once and she became his pupil, learning many of his skills and powers. Finally, however, it was said that she tired of his advances, and turned his magic against him, imprisoning him within a cave, its entrance sealed by a great stone.*

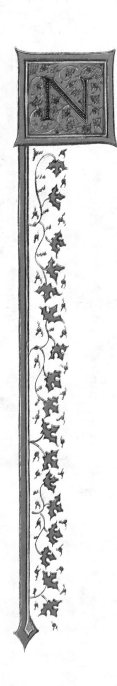

Name
Address

Telephone

Name
Address

Telephone

Name
Address

Telephone

Name
Address

Telephone

Name
Address

Telephone

Name

Address

Telephone

Name

Address

Telephone

Name

Address

Telephone

Name

Address

Telephone

Name

Address

Telephone

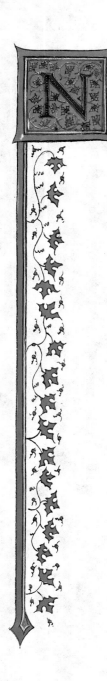

Name

Address

Telephone

Name

Address

Telephone

Name

Address

Telephone

Name

Address

Telephone

Name

Address

Telephone

Name

Address

Telephone

Name

Address

Telephone

Name

Address

Telephone

Name

Address

Telephone

Name

Address

Telephone

ORKNEY. *The Orkney Isles played a large part in the history of Arthur's realm. Lot, King of Lothian and Orkney, led a rebel alliance against Arthur. Lot's wife, Morgause, Arthur's half-sister, became the mother of Mordred, who was destined to bring about the downfall of the Round Table. Morgause's other sons – Gawain, Gareth, Gaheries and Agravaine – were all important knights at the Arthurian court.*

Name
Address

Telephone
Name
Address

Telephone
Name
Address

Telephone
Name
Address

Telephone
Name
Address

Telephone

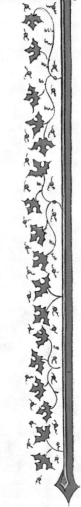

Name

Address

Telephone

Name

Address

Telephone

Name

Address

Telephone

Name

Address

Telephone

Name

Address

Telephone

Name

Address

Telephone

Name

Address

Telephone

Name

Address

Telephone

Name

Address

Telephone

Name

Address

Telephone

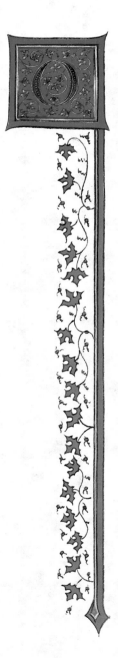

Name

Address

Telephone

Name

Address

Telephone

Name

Address

Telephone

Name

Address

Telephone

Name

Address

Telephone

PALOMIDES. The son of King Astlabor the Saracen, Palomides was the only non-Christian knight to sit at the Round Table. By all accounts a mighty warrior, he was Tristan's bitter rival for the love of Isolt of Ireland. After the death of King Pellinor he took up the search for the Questing Beast, a strange creature with the head of a serpent, the body of a leopard and the feet of a hart. Palomides later became a faithful supporter of Lancelot.

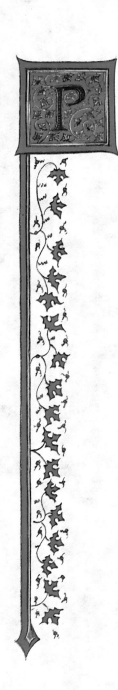

Name

Address

Telephone

Name

Address

Telephone

Name

Address

Telephone

Name

Address

Telephone

Name

Address

Telephone

Name

Address

Telephone

◇

Name

Address

Telephone

◇

Name

Address

Telephone

◇

Name

Address

Telephone

◇

Name

Address

Telephone

◇

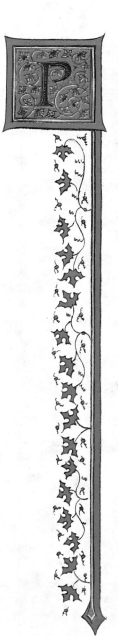

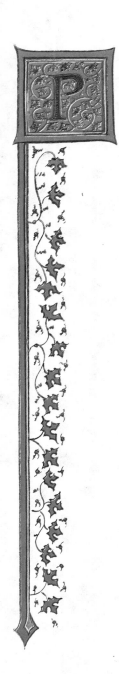

Name

Address

Telephone

Name

Address

Telephone

Name

Address

Telephone

Name

Address

Telephone

Name

Address

Telephone

Name

Address

Telephone

Name

Address

Telephone

Name

Address

Telephone

Name

Address

Telephone

Name

Address

Telephone

QUEST OF THE WHITE HART. *This was the first Quest of the Round Table Fellowship after its foundation by Arthur and Merlin. A white hart fled through the great hall of Camelot, followed by a hound and a lady. A strange knight carried off the lady and her dog. So three of Arthur's newest knights were set the challenge of finding out the hart, the dog, the lady and the knight.*

Name

Address

Telephone

Name

Address

Telephone

Name

Address

Telephone

Name

Address

Telephone

Name

Address

Telephone

Name

Address

Telephone

Name

Address

Telephone

Name

Address

Telephone

Name

Address

Telephone

Name

Address

Telephone

Name

Address

Telephone

Name

Address

Telephone

Name

Address

Telephone

Name

Address

Telephone

Name

Address

Telephone

Name

Address

Telephone

Name

Address

Telephone

Name

Address

Telephone

Name

Address

Telephone

Name

Address

Telephone

THE ROUND TABLE. *Soon after his coronation, Arthur took Guinevere for his wife, the daughter of Leodegraunce of Camiliarde. One of her wedding gifts was a great round table which could seat 150 people. This had been created by Merlin, in token of the roundness of the world. At Merlin's instigation, Arthur now founded a Fellowship of the best knights in the world, who sat at the table as equals, to relate their adventures and to go forth through the land to right wrongs.*

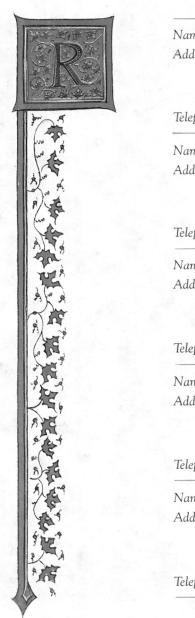

Name

Address

Telephone

Name

Address

Telephone

Name

Address

Telephone

Name

Address

Telephone

Name

Address

Telephone

Name

Address

Telephone

Name

Address

Telephone

Name

Address

Telephone

Name

Address

Telephone

Name

Address

Telephone

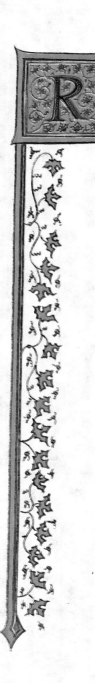

Name

Address

Telephone

Name

Address

Telephone

Name

Address

Telephone

Name

Address

Telephone

Name

Address

Telephone

Name

Address

Telephone

Name

Address

Telephone

Name

Address

Telephone

Name

Address

Telephone

Name

Address

Telephone

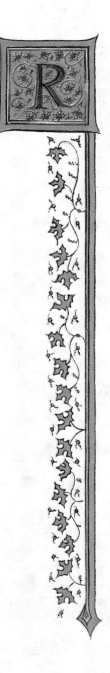

SURLUSE. A kingdom to the west of Arthur's, Surluse was ruled over by the hot-headed but chivalrous Prince Galehaut. Galehaut made war upon Arthur, who dispatched Lancelot to put down the revolt. So impressed was the Prince by his adversary's chivalrous behaviour that he surrendered to him. The two men became close friends, and Galehaut sought to honour his friend by arranging for him to be alone with Guinevere for the first time during a visit to Surluse.

Name

Address

Telephone

Name

Address

Telephone

Name

Address

Telephone

Name

Address

Telephone

Name

Address

Telephone

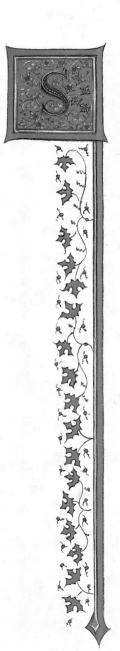

Name

Address

Telephone

Name

Address

Telephone

Name

Address

Telephone

Name

Address

Telephone

Name

Address

Telephone

Name

Address

Telephone

Name

Address

Telephone

Name

Address

Telephone

Name

Address

Telephone

Name

Address

Telephone

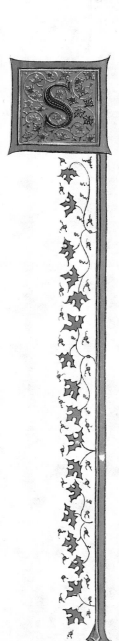

Name

Address

Telephone

Name

Address

Telephone

Name

Address

Telephone

Name

Address

Telephone

Name

Address

Telephone

Name

Address

Telephone

Name

Address

Telephone

Name

Address

Telephone

Name

Address

Telephone

Name

Address

Telephone

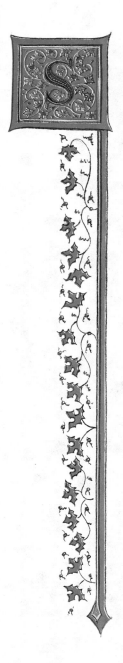

TRISTAN. *Son of King Meliodas and Queen Elizabeth of Lyonesse, Tristan became the champion of his uncle, King Mark of Cornwall, by defeating the gigantic Irish knight known as Morhold and journeying to Ireland to fetch the Princess Isolt to be his uncle's bride. On the return voyage, however, the pair fell in love, and entered upon a long and dangerous affair which ended in both their deaths. For a time, Tristan was recognized as one of the greatest of the Round Table Knights.*

Name
Address

Telephone

Name
Address

Telephone

Name
Address

Telephone

Name
Address

Telephone

Name
Address

Telephone

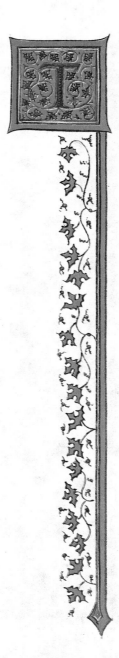

Name

Address

Telephone

Name

Address

Telephone

Name

Address

Telephone

Name

Address

Telephone

Name

Address

Telephone

Name

Address

Telephone

Name

Address

Telephone

Name

Address

Telephone

Name

Address

Telephone

Name

Address

Telephone

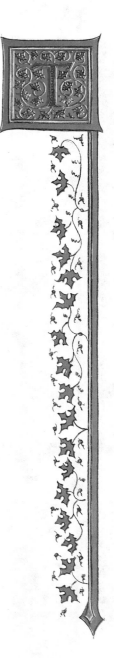

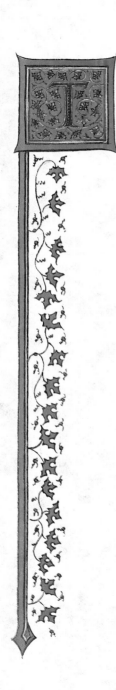

Name

Address

Telephone

Name

Address

Telephone

Name

Address

Telephone

Name

Address

Telephone

Name

Address

Telephone

VORTIGERN. *Usurping the rightful heirs to the throne and styling himself High King, Vortigern was much hated. The Princes Ambrosius and Uther soon raised an army against Vortigern, forcing him to flee. In an isolated location in Wales he consulted the child Merlin as to the reason why his castle would not stand. The prophet revealed that two dragons fought beneath the hill, and went on to predict the usurper's own imminent death.*

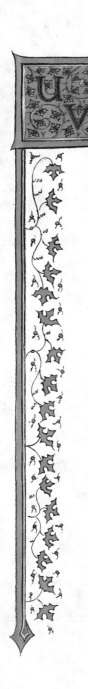

Name

Address

Telephone

Name

Address

Telephone

Name

Address

Telephone

Name

Address

Telephone

Name

Address

Telephone

Name

Address

Telephone

Name

Address

Telephone

Name

Address

Telephone

Name

Address

Telephone

Name

Address

Telephone

Name

Address

Telephone

Name

Address

Telephone

Name

Address

Telephone

Name

Address

Telephone

Name

Address

Telephone

Name

Address

Telephone

Name

Address

Telephone

Name

Address

Telephone

Name

Address

Telephone

Name

Address

Telephone

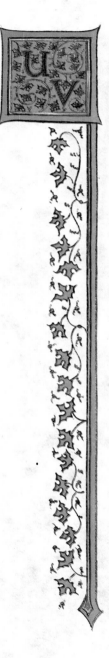

THE WOUNDED KING. At the heart of the mysteries of the Grail lay King Pelles, suffering from an unhealing wound which could be remedied only by a knight successful in the Quest. Many came to his castle and attempted to heal him; but in the end it was his own nephew, Sir Perceval, who made him whole by touching the wound with the tip of the sacred lance, believed to be the lance which pierced Christ's side during the Crucifixion.

Name

Address

Telephone

Name

Address

Telephone

Name

Address

Telephone

Name

Address

Telephone

Name

Address

Telephone

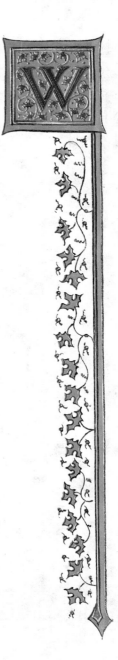

Name

Address

Telephone

Name

Address

Telephone

Name

Address

Telephone

Name

Address

Telephone

Name

Address

Telephone

Name

Address

Telephone

Name

Address

Telephone

Name

Address

Telephone

Name

Address

Telephone

Name

Address

Telephone

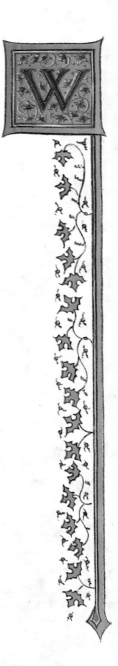

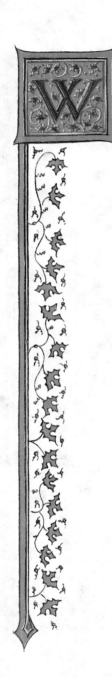

Name

Address

Telephone

Name

Address

Telephone

Name

Address

Telephone

Name

Address

Telephone

Name

Address

Telephone

Not all his magic could prevent Merlin from being caught and imprisoned by the wily lady Nimue, whom he so loved that he gave her many of his secrets, until she grew so powerful that she was able to imprison him in a cave from which he could not escape. In this medieval picture the cave has become a more conventional prison cell, from the window of which the mage addresses Sir Gawain with his final message to the King.

Name

Address

Telephone

Name

Address

Telephone

Name

Address

Telephone

Name

Address

Telephone

Name

Address

Telephone

Name

Address

Telephone

Name

Address

Telephone

Name

Address

Telephone

Name

Address

Telephone

Name

Address

Telephone

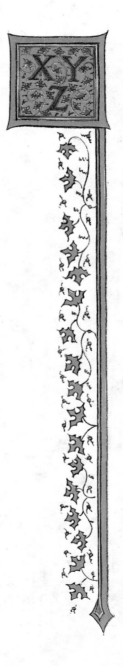

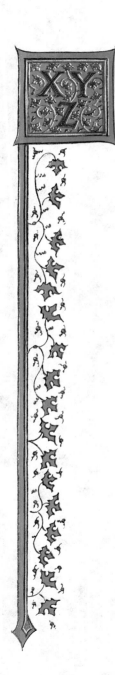

Name

Address

Telephone

Name

Address

Telephone

Name

Address

Telephone

Name

Address

Telephone

Name

Address

Telephone

Name

Address

Telephone

Name

Address

Telephone

Name

Address

Telephone

Name

Address

Telephone

Name

Address

Telephone

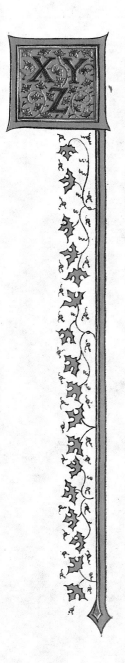

Acknowledgements

The Archbishop of Canterbury and Trustees of the Lambeth Palace Library: p 16, MS 6 f54v; p113, MS 6 f43v. Bibliothèque Nationale, Paris: p22, MS Fr 343 f59v; p54, MS Fr 343 f61v; p60, MS Fr 343 f7; p65, MS Fr 119 f312v; p87, MS Fr 99 f143; p97, MS Fr 343 f3; p102, MS Fr 118 f219v; p118t, MS Fr 342 f84v; p118b, MS Fr 12577 f18v. The Bodleian Library, Oxford: p44, MS Douce 215 f14r; p82, MS Rawlinson Q.b.6. f267r; p123, MS Douce 178 f411v. The British Library, London: p6, MS Add. 10294 f87v; p28, MS Add. 10294 f94; p71, MS Add. 12228 f202v; p77, MS Add. 38117 f185; p92, MS Add. 10294 f45v. Österreichische Nationalbibliothek, Vienna: p11, MS 2537; p49, MS 2537; p108, MS 2737. The Pierpont Morgan Library, New York: p38, MS 805 f48. Princeton University Library: p33, Garrett MS 125 f52r.